# THE URBANIZED NIGERIAN

Economic expansion and improved standards of living are reflected in a big boom in the building industry and large-scale urban development throughout Nigeria. Architects: Nickson & Borys & Partners. The author worked on the design drawings as an assistant architect in the summer of 1961.

An example of indigenous Nigerian architecture, showing decorated walls.

# The Urbanized Nigerian

## AN EXAMINATION OF THE AFRICAN
## AND HIS NEW ENVIRONMENT

*by*

## Theophilus Adelodun Okin, M.Sc.

Urban Design Consultant,
City of New York Housing
and Development Administration

*An Exposition-University Book*

EXPOSITION PRESS          NEW YORK

# EXPOSITION PRESS INC.

50 Jericho Turnpike        Jericho, New York 11753

### FIRST EDITION

LIBRARY OF CONGRESS CATALOGUE CARD NUMBER: 68-24881

EP 46833

Dedicated to Beatrice Oriade,

Mary Olorunsola, and Isaiah Akinjokun Okin,

and the entire Okin family

and

To Africa and the other developing areas of the world

*Prefactory comment by His Excellency, Chief S. O. Adebo, Ambassador and Permanent Representative of Nigeria at the United Nations; Under-Secretary and Executive Director-designate of the United Nations Institute for Training and Research*

I appreciate the compliment that Theo Okin has done me in asking me to record a prefactory comment on this book, since he must be aware that, unlike Eric Carlson (who is writing the Foreword), I am not an expert in the field of housing. I am complying with pleasure.

I am doing so because, for one thing, this gives me an opportunity to join in paying tribute to Mr. Okin for venturing into print on a subject of this kind and doing it in a courageous, even provocative, manner. If he succeeds only in provoking others, professional and non-professional, to take him up on some of his strong positions, he will have rendered a worthy enough service to the cause of housing development in developing countries.

That cause should profit greatly from a frank dialogue between persons interested in the different aspects of this subject. It is not only governments—whose inadequate leadership Okin criticises—that need to be persuaded to show greater concern. If there is to be improvement in the national performance in this as in other areas of development activity, the interest of all the citizenry must be engaged. For this reason I hope that as many Nigerians as possible, and of course other Africans, will read this book.

S. O. ADEBO

# Foreword

In this little book the author has attempted an enormous task, to put before us in simple terms some of the universalities of the urbanization process, as illustrated through his own knowledge and experiences of the African scene, particularly Nigeria. Highly trained and qualified as an architect, the author has been the recipient of a number of special prizes and awards. He is a registered architect in Nigeria and has been engaged in a number of important projects in his own country as well as in the United States and Europe.

The book poses the dilemma of the current urbanization scene in Africa, particularly the basic problem of the adjustment of traditional ways of family living to modern urban life. The author provides suggestions for physical planning and design factors, and for ways of minimizing the spread of squatters. He points to measures which should be taken to deal with the problems of urbanization, taking into account the realities of the present stages of economic development. It is clear that the areas of concern described in this book are worthy of much greater attention than they have received to date from the professionals and government authorities charged with responsibility for design and construction of housing and community facilities in the newly emerging countries of the world. A fresh look at the potentials of existing resources and the possibilities of indigenous building materials and methods can help to provide family and community living patterns of the future which will foster a more rational transition to modernization in this sector rather than total disruption of the whole society as so often takes place.

ERIC CARLSON
*Chief, Housing Section,*
*United Nations, New York*

# Acknowledgment

It was a combined effort of Mr. David J. Vickery, Head of the Faculty of Architecture, Ahmadu Bello University, Zaria, Nigeria; my Year Master, Mr. J. C. Moughton; and a visiting lecturer, Mr. Gerald B. Dix, that convinced me to think of attempting postgraduate studies overseas. Their advice has materialized in my diverse and deeper involvement in professional practice, graduate studies, research, teaching, and consultancy in the field of architecture, housing, and urban planning. I therefore, in this little book, want to express my gratitude to Messrs. Vickery, Moughton, and Dix, and to other staff members of my alma mater, for their encouragement and assistance.

At the Graduate School of Architecture, Planning and Housing of Columbia University, I was to learn more about my profession. Columbia's school is renowned as a meeting ground for top professors with conflicting and controversial opinions and philosophies. The graduate student discovers that he is a swimmer in rough waters and strong currents that demand lusty sinews for survival. Here, professors' ideas range from pure functionalism in design to the weird confines of the abstract philosophies of extentialism. Both extremities caught my fancy; and I must mention that I am greatly indebted to Professors Victor Christ-Janer, Arthur E. Bye, Jr., and Felix McCormick, of Teachers College. Listening to lectures of Professors Eric Carlson and Charles Abrams, both United Nations experts on housing in the developing countries, was quite refreshing. From them I developed the philosophy based on "realism" of events in developing countries. Sometimes I disagreed with Professors Abrams and Kenneth Smith (Dean of the school), but the friction each time led to an improvement in my sense of constructive criticism. I think that I was fortunate to have the opportunity of coming face to face with such stalwarts, and to argue, reason, and discuss urban environmental problems with them.

My travels overseas have brought me in direct contact with experts like Dr. Otto Koenigsberger of the London Architectural Association School of Tropical Architecture, and Professor R. G. Hopkinson, Head of the Department of Environmental Design, University College, London University. My brief exciting discussions with them have enriched my experience; and I hope this book will be of interest to them.

My extensive travels and my exposure to the academic influence of the distinguished staff of England's leading Liverpool University School of Architecture have helped me tremendously. I am very grateful to Professor R. Gardner-Medwin, Dr. Quentin-Hughes, and Mr. Francis M. Jones, Director of the Housing Research and Development Group. I spent a productive time doing housing research and development under the supervision of Mr. Jones. Under him I developed my ideas fully, to the point of becoming convinced that I should no longer drag my feet in facing the mountainous challenge of publishing a thought-provoking book in America. This takes more courage than one might suppose; and I am greatly indebted to Mr. Jones, and Professor Gardner-Medwin.

I shall ever be grateful to the Government of Nigeria, Columbia University, and the African-American Institute, which have provided me with graduate research and travel grants, and fellowships.

My special thanks go to His Excellency, Chief S. O. Adebo, Ambassador and Permanent Representative of Nigeria at the United Nations, and to Mr. Eric Carlson, Chief, Housing Section of the United Nations, New York, for the pains they have taken in reading the manuscript and for their invaluable comments.

I wish also to convey my thanks to one of my former teachers, Mr. Kenneth H. Murta of Sheffield University, for the use of illustrations from his B. Arch. thesis.

T. A. O.

# CONTENTS

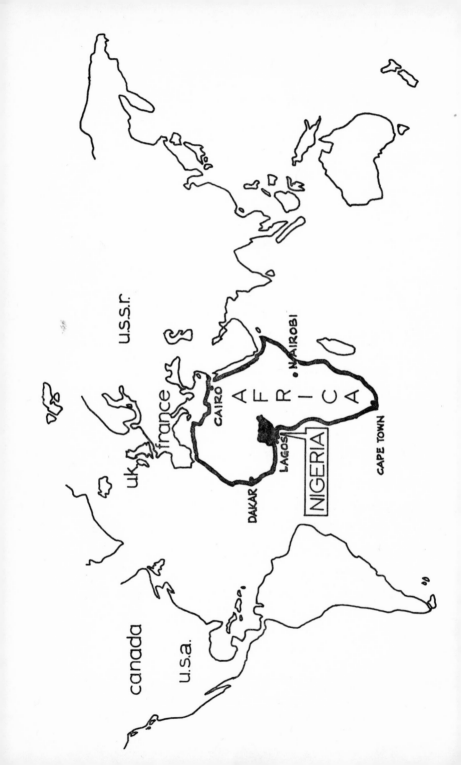

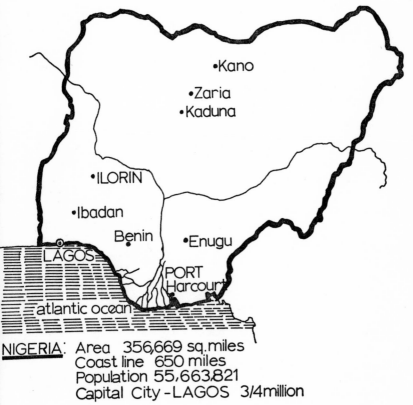

•Kano

•Zaria
•Kaduna

•ILORIN

•Ibadan

Benin•    •Enugu

LAGOS

PORT
Harcourt

atlantic ocean

NIGERIA: Area   356,669 sq.miles
         Coast line   650 miles
         Population 55,663,821
         Capital City - LAGOS  3/4million

# Introduction

## A Continent in Transition

Africa is a continent large enough to contain the United States three times over. It is a conglomerate of old and new cities, from Timbuktu, the old Saharan "El Dorado" gold market to Dakar, the glittering jewel, the Paris, of Africa, or to both old and new intermixed, as exemplified in Cairo and other Nile cities. It is a continent in which the magic word *progress* is encountered everywhere—spoken or represented in terms of physical environment. It is a continent suddenly awakening from an ages-long deep, Rip van Winkle slumber and trying to catch up with a fast-moving jet and sputnik age. It is still half asleep—more correctly perhaps, sleepwalking—but behold, its inhabitants are swept up in the race! It is a continent chewing on too big a mouthful but not daring to let go lest it lose its meal forever and starve. This is Africa—where things are happening amidst the booms of gunfire from military coups d'état.

It is a place where the sounds of "Harambe!" "Uhuru!" "Freedom!" ring loud and clear. It is the locale of the stately ancient pyramids of Egypt and the modern glass skyscrapers of Nairobi, and yet of the lowly, but pleasant and dignifying, indigenous African mud hut. The physical environment for the most part has changed but little since the wildest of beasts roamed freely in the jungles and over the plains.

In the jumble of diverse activities, of fervent movements

for political power and education and all else, the indigenous owner of the land, the African, is as confused as ever. He is being urbanized at such a breath-taking pace that he is faced with the dilemma of choosing between the old and the new, or even abandoning both, or combining both to evolve his own unique urban environment, as the Brazilians evolved their own refined tropical architecture. It is still too early to judge, or to forecast a direction; but it is well to reveal the African's state of mind, and perhaps some expert opinion can help. Help indeed is needed, especially in housing and urban planning. Even with the African heritage of traditional community living and local government and administration, Africans cannot resist urbanization as they have resisted progressive forces from time immemorial.

Foreign experts in Africa suffer from great handicaps in performing their highly desirable functions. Granted that they are people of immense experience and knowledge in their various professions and that their performance within their own countries or similar countries may be very efficient, their tasks nevertheless are certainly more difficult when they are called upon to assist countries with markedly different social, economic, political, and environmental backgrounds.

This statement is valid even for relatively advanced countries; for example, an expert from capitalist America whose service is needed in communist Russia faces a more difficult task than he would in England or Canada. If we can succeed in imagining the situation in this simple case, we need not tax our imaginations so much to visualize the difficulty of the foreign expert, be he American, Russian, English, French, or German, who is called upon to help in any developing country, especially a tropical country in Africa, Latin America, or Asia. The inhabitants of these developing continents have very different, distinct cultures and civilizations let alone different physical environments characterized by earthquakes in Turkey, monsoon rains in India, deserts in Algeria and Mali, and impregnable tropical forests in the Congo, Nigeria, and the Amazons, to mention a few.

To help the Africans, the experts have to see Africans as they truly are. This essay attempts, therefore, to outline several factors which require particular attention from the housing and urban planning experts. These factors constitute the rudiments of the housing ailment of African cities.

Cities are for people; hence the person—the individual self—is important. This fact underlies the dilemma experienced by the urbanized African.

## The Physical Background

Many African proverbs reflect the dos and don'ts of African communities. The proverbs exist in the form of similes and idioms using common living and non-living objects, including people, for description. Like many other peoples, Africans prefer to express their opinions in concrete material terms that appeal to their physical senses. For example, the almighty African gods Sango (God of Thunder) and Soponna (God of Smallpox) are believed to be present during rains and epidemics, respectively, in actual visible forms. Thus a public personality with a fierce look and a roaring, terrifying voice is reverently called "Sango."

Again, a hen collects her chicks under her wings when a hungry hawk dives for a catch amongst them or when the weather is inclement—rains, storms, the scorching tropical sun. The hen thus contains her chicks, her wings affording protection and safety while the danger lasts. In turn the chicks feel secure and guarded from the view of unfriendly intruders. The materials of containment in this instance are

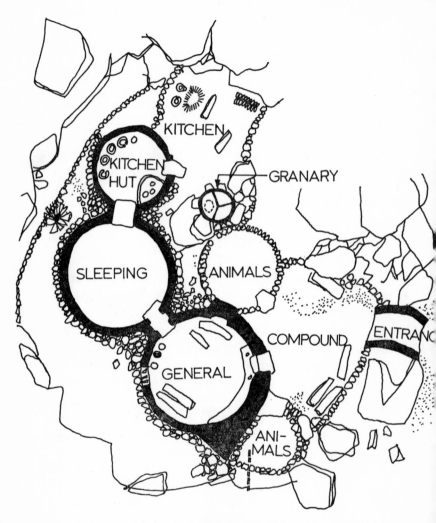

A HIGI COMPOUND

the wings of the mother hen. But to guarantee adequate protection the wings must have the following characteristics:

a) *flexibility*—the capability of stretching their fibers to cover up the chicks
b) *know-how*—the technical art of stretching in instantaneous response to danger
c) *size*—suitable to cover up the numerous chicks to be cared for

All three characteristics help to develop in the chicks the actual feeling of security and containment.

In terms of physical environment, the element of containment was achieved in Africa's history in several interesting ways for purposes of defense and protection.

SCALE. Control of village and city sizes was practiced, but there were no written laws that controlled population size. Population was usually left to take care of itself, and it seemed to have a built-in control within its growth cycle. Surplus population in the historic African village settlement usually gave rise to the community substances requisite to constitute the nucleus of a new village. For instance, the successful and powerful families with extended units and clans (there could be as many as two hundred people in an extended family unit) could desire more agricultural land and the administrative power to choose their own village chief, and therefore would decide to establish a new village. Several such family units might join to create a village on a much larger scale. But one point was obvious: the smaller the new village, the greater was its dependence on the mother village for mutual assistance, especially for defense of the daughter village. The villages were usually established firmly on the physical design principles of containment which had emerged in practice from human intuition.

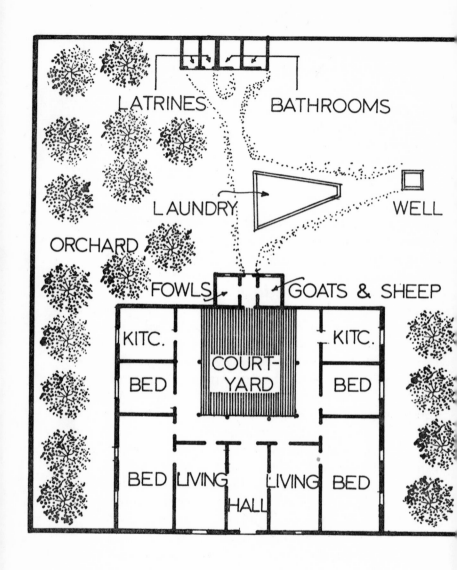

IMPROVED TRADITIONAL HOUSE PLAN

PHYSICAL LIMITS. Village boundaries were defined strictly on the basis of pedestrian orientation, with natural landmarks, such as hills, rivers, and streams, acting as deterrents to enemies, and tall trees acting as watchtowers and defense outposts from which arrows were shot.

LAYOUT. The layout plan was informal, with huts and houses and barns placed at random around courtyards, which were used for recreation, storytelling, daily domestic activities, and such home industries as weaving and smithing; and also around the chief's house. It was usually characterized by curving footpaths leading to the entrances of the various shelters.

In brief, traditional planning was characterized by these factors:

organic design
containment
compactness
pedestrian-oriented traffic
self-sufficiency
communication at the personal level
protection
recreation
scale
climatic comfort
close social interaction
flexibility for future expansion

## The Scarcity of Statistics

The mature scholar who weaves into his research a scarlet thread by numerical symbols and analysis to brighten his study does so with little fuss or intellectual ostentation, and with him none should quarrel. The results of his labors clearly demonstrate the importance of quantitative methods. In Africa this scholar is handicapped by lack of sufficient and reliable statistics, especially in West Africa. The fact is that this is one of Africa's distinct difficulties. African problems—housing and urbanization not excepted—are in rhythmic limbo with the "uncertain realities" of African community ailments. "The comparative absence of statistics is a fact of life in Nigeria, and one must accept it as a regrettable but unavoidable reality for a number of years to come."[1]

Even worse is the increasing difficulty imposed by the civil wars under current military regimes.

How far can an expert's effort be successful in view of the shortage of statistical data? This is obviously a big headache.

Government departments usually resort to crude statistical methods which sometimes result in grave errors. For instance, the crude death rate in Lagos, Nigeria, averaged for 1955–59 was officially given as 12.8 per thousand. This figure, when compared with the figures of 12.0 and 9.3 per thousand respectively for Great Britain and the United States, with their high standards of nutrition and medical care and highly creditable pattern of death control, and in view of the lower standards of housing, sanitation, and acute shortage of doctors and hospitals in a developing city like Lagos, is incredible. The figures for Ghana 22.7, the Ivory Coast 28.0, and Guinea 40.0 per thousand appeared more correct and helped to reveal the far-out error of Lagos' figure.

Colonial-era censuses, which were based on taxation, land acquisition, and military conscription and to which many Africans were reluctant to give honest responses for

---

[1] *Nigerian Geographical Association Journal*, June 1966, p. 13.

economic reasons, have given way to more modern census techniques consonant with the attainment of political independence. The dogma of "one man, one vote" has changed the outlook considerably. But an African country is still a long way from adopting most of the modern techniques used in the United States, Britain, or Russia, even with the aid of computers.

One may hazard a guess that there are more people in Africa than the official census figures indicate; therefore one can envisage a bigger role for planners and social workers. These should work more at the local level, try to obtain an exact picture of the patterns of thinking, behavior, and experience of the commoners at grass-root levels, since they are planning for the "people." Efforts should be made to interpret the patterns in quantitative and qualitative terms useful for the statistics which are vital for the planning process. The professional training of architects, planners, social workers, geographers, etcetera, for Africa should aim at instilling a thorough understanding of the vast scope of the problems and of the objectives to be sought in overcoming them. This idea will emphasize field work at local and regional levels. Simple methods for the assembly and interpretation of statistical data should be taught.

# The Dilemma and Suggestions
## for Improvement
................................................................

### Adjustment to Urban Life

A random sampling of ninety persons were interviewed in Sapele, Nigeria's third largest port and the hub of its timber and rubber industries. The following questionnaire was posed verbally:

Do you feel very much attached to this community?
Are the people here generally critical of you and unfriendly?
Have you found life better than you expected?
Do many people think themselves too nice for you?
Would you like to settle in this community for the rest of
    your life until retirement age?
Are trustworthy friends hard to find here?
If ever you moved away from this city, would you ever like
    to return to it?
Does everyone here try to cheat you?

The answers were rated as "Certainly not," "No," "Not decided," and "Yes."[2]

The results yielded the opinions of two distinct groups of people: (*a*) members of clan/village unions, (*b*) non-members of unions.

------

[2] *Nigerian Journal of Economic and Social Studies,* March 1967, p. 55.

It was found that 64 of ($a$) had a mean score of urban adjustment of 19.5, while 25 of ($b$) had 17.2. It was observed that (1) members of clan/village unions were significantly better adjusted to the urban milieu than non-members; (2) urban adjustment is a function of length of urban residence.

A brief explanation of this is that clan unions have functionally replaced the extended family units within whose tradition of social co-operation the migrants were brought up. The unions function mainly as socio-economic and psychological security, and they virtually guarantee guardianship from shelter to employment during the early, most critical stage of settling in. They speed up the rate of adjustment to the problems of the city. Once the immigrant becomes urbanized, after two years, he needs less help from the unions, and at that stage be begins to get involved in the real dilemma of urbanization—making a choice between two or more worlds. The reasons behind the unions' success can be seen in the contents of their constitutions, which state the guidelines of the unions' objectives—the disciplinary clauses, which impose fines on offenders; the social-control clauses; and the financial clauses, the backbone of effectuation of programs—and in the actual procedure of union meetings.

The clan unions directly determine the individual's experience of urban life from the time he first enters the extratribal community of his new city environment.

The unions create a new solidarity with which the immigrant can identifiy himself, so that he reacts less violently to the tensions inherent in the new society. The immigrant, immediately drawing from the experience of his forerunners, feels less isolated as the traditional social support and control continues to be available to him.

On the other hand, non-members, by reason of their constant need to grapple with diverse and strange social

## CLAN/VILLAGE UNION FUNCTIONS

Clan/Village Unions

| The Union and the Individual | | The Union and Society | |
| --- | --- | --- | --- |
| Dictionary of urban life | Socio-economic and psychological security for immigrants (functionally replace the extended family in creating new solidarities) | Organs of social control | Agencies of development (initiate/ sponsor development projects, e.g., colleges, churches, etc.) |

problems in an unfamiliar setting, are apt to remain frustrated for many years.

Thus clan/student/tribal/trade unions are valuable local tools of progress and development. These organizations operate mini-planning and mini-development machineries at the community level that are highly disciplined and effective, and reach the pulse of the commoners better than anything else. I believe that they can be useful tools in the urban planning process. Their services, co-operation, participation, and involvement must be enlisted if good surgery is to be performed on the "sick" African cities (especially in Nigeria) to get rid of squatting. Foreign experts should give particular attention to how this can best be carried out. The unions know much about the dilemma, the confusion, the agonies, of the urbanized and the urbanizing African.

Unfortunately, the unions' might is limited by the limited funds at their disposal; and they are not therefore well equipped to finance housing projects of appreciable scale, beyond the mere hospitality residence provision for new immigrants. At first, clan unions serve as ethnic pockets which prevent rural detachment. Gradually, however, these unions make urban setting gratifying to the newcomer by:

a) Facilitating adjustment
b) Increasing involvement in urban life
c) Reinforcing urban adjustment
d) Increasing rural detachment, i.e., detachment from traditional society and/or way of life
e) Placing less emphasis on membership in clan unions
f) Placing more emphasis on membership in recreational clubs and other "specialized" unions, e.g., trade unions

This progress is valid when making efforts to house new immigrants, in order to obtain controlled accommodation and housing, stage by stage, until the immigrants finally are permanently settled in. Thus the spread of squatters can be checked; squatter physical environment can be planned, and renewed from time to time, in far better, adjustable sanitary conditions.

## Family Planning

This concerns the African women more than the men, for the ladies have assumed increasing authority at home. Ask women, "How many children do you desire to have?" and answers will range from "between four and six" for those with university, college teacher-training, or secondary-school education to "as many as God provides" for the illiterate. Education is a strong deciding element of their reasoning faculty. Furthermore, the more educated women are more concerned with the quality of education their children receive as well as with material and social satisfaction.

Africans, male and female, under present inadequate economic capability still regard children as the surest means of insurance for old-age retirement. Children are by custom and tradition supposed to cater to their parents when the parents become too old to work, say about fifty-five to sixty years of age. This is a moral obligation which Africans strictly observe. So the greater the number of surviving children an old couple have, the greater the contribution the couple receive from their children to live a pleasant, untroubled life when they retire. It is therefore not surprising that couples desire to protect themselves thus against the future, and earnestly pray to give birth to more children. As the standard of living soars all over Africa, a couple's pension or savings may not be worth enough to ensure the purchasing power that will last them until their death; such an uncertainty is counterbalanced by financial assistance from children.

The use of contraceptives for family planning is influenced by education, income, occupation, and religious belief. So long as there is food in abundance, as in Nigeria and Ghana, where agricultural products form 80 per cent of the exports, the citizens do not panic because of overpopulation, as in India. But one should not underestimate the power behind women's decision in such a matter, and so it is well for social workers, planners, and educators to start working on the women now, in order to have them effectually persuaded ten to twenty years hence. Otherwise sharp population explosion will be the headache then.

## Development Projects: politics, housing, and the cash pinch

Private developers, corporations, some government departments, and local authorities have alienated land for specific projects without sufficient study of the consequences to the rest of the metropolis. The result is (1) overexpenditure not initially provided for in the budget, (2) inability to complete projects, (3) an increasing number of unfinished projects, and (4) an increasing number of overlapping brought-forward projects. This shortsighted planning and poor programing usually becomes a backlash in community and national politics. It is not unusual for the reputation of a notable politician to wane while that of a budding politician waxes stronger because of these projects. By and large, the citizens in and around cities understand the game, and very soon join the bandwagon and demand fantastic promises for the establishment of new housing, industrial projects, or even a stadium, or the completion of existing projects, in return for support at the ballot box.

In a country where an insufficiency of money is apparent, and the plague of defective planning, though disastrous, is absorbed by the struggling unbanized citizen with a mere shrug and henceforth overlooked in the name of progress, with the characteristic "What can I do, after all? . . . You have to shuffle along with the general public attitude," it is easy to see that the individual urbanized citizen is a confused person being torn apart by multifarious handicaps in his national environment. Typical examples of unsuccessful projects may be found in Lagos, Nigeria—the national stadium, the second mainland bridge, and the inadequate housing estates at Surulere (New Lagos).

At the community level, a level which petty representatives canvass for votes for seats in the local council, the urbanized citizen's domestic grievances receive more political attention—not usually for the better, of course, but rather to be used as a political football and as a source of inspiration in the topsy-turvy rhythm of creating political slogans that touch the people with appeals to which they are most sensitive. The politicians who build their platforms around the complaints usually emerge successful at the polls.

What are the complaints? The first is about poor housing, the citizen's inability to buy land because he cannot afford it out of his meager savings—the land is too expensive, he says; and also because of the inevitable web of red tape he has to pass through in order to buy a plot, if he is rich enough. The maze of red tape, for instance in the large cities of Nigeria—Lagos, Ibadan, Enugu, Port Harcourt—may exhaust his small savings through tips, or "dash." If he is to buy a plot costing £1 a square yard from an organization, he must allow at least 10 per cent for tips, and some extras for surveyor's fees, lawyer's fees, approval of drawings, and other transactions. If he is to buy the land from private owners, the percentage may skyrocket to about 25 per cent, with the delicate risk of being swindled without owning any land in the end.

In short, the urbanized citizen must have greater savings in order to acquire land. He must persevere through an abominable purchasing process. He must have determination and iron will. He must possess a thorough understanding of the community he lives in. Socially, this requires that he be a good mixer capable of making friends and knowing the right persons in authority connected with his objective. In Western countries this is not easy, but in Africa it is quite simple. In Lagos and Accra, for example, frequent outdoor social parties, ceremonies, and meetings at night clubs produce the swinging atmosphere, enlivened by the "Highlife" or the authentic native music of "Apala" and "Gangan," that makes extremely easy the introduction of the needy man to the needed man. Uninvited guests are welcomed with free beer and palm wine and the friendliest smiles ever. It is conventional in the community that the sounds of music quickly formulate the basis of social intercourse at all levels. His natural way of life distinguishes the African as a hospitable person in this modern world. His problem lies not in making social contacts, as is usually the case with non-Africans abroad, but in obtaining ready "cash" to buy what he wants. Money is scarce in Africa, and that is a fact!

The African city's social standards are nowadays becoming highly demanding. They tax the patience, the honor, the prestige, of the individual urbanized African severely. His employment at a better wage in the city is almost completely negated by social demands, with the result that he finds himself trapped in a continual, never-ending struggle to own his own shelter, improved household furniture, equipment, etcetera. Superficially his income may be high, but the prices of goods have risen correspondingly, as if to challenge his audacity at spending. Thus as the standard of living improves, he finds his domestic responsibilities more and more difficult to fulfill, and his chances of owning a small modern house far more remote than fifteen years ago. Since it is not very dignifying to build in the traditional way, with cheap traditional materials, many of the elite group are reluctant to build "outdated" houses, and instead yearn for the day they can enjoy nice little modern houses.

There seem to be two distinct categories of urbanized Africans: the elite—educated, of high, middle, and low income groups; and the illiterate—uneducated, born and bred in the city or having migrated there to seek their fortune.

The elite category can be summed up as the group with steady employment and salary income, and therefore able to afford better housing. This group looks for quality in housing and sets the pace of advancement and progress in the community. From this group comes most of the demand for the better standard types of housing—the modern houses built of concrete blocks, with asbestos-cement roofing, glass windows, and steel door and window framing instead of timber framing. This group is mainly responsible for the ever soaring cost of S.R.O.'s (single-room occupancies), apartments (flats), and bungalows and mansions.

On the other hand, the illiterate group, owing to their strict economic limitations and the accompanying unsanitary overcrowding, are responsible for the spread of squatters' shacks and river pollution.

Of great significance is the fact that the elite group is usually a very small percentage of the city population. The political implication of this is that the illustrious elite politician has to go to the squatters, hobnob with the squatter settement, in order to secure enough votes in an election to gain a majority. The "one man, one vote" regulation has actually centralized political power in the squatters. An example of this is seen in Lagos Central Island and Ebute-Metta. Therefore, even though an urbanized African may be a squatter and confused, he cheerfully comforts himself that he is reckoned with in the community: he is a member of the significant low-income squatter group!

It will be good if experts observe this prevalent political strategy and map out a way of using it to the benefit of urban planning and housing.

Wole Soyinka, the well-known Nigerian writer, once said: "It takes only three or four years to create that true 'high-breed' . . . the 'Johnny-just-come' squatter from rural Nigeria to Lagos city. But after a while he is unmistakable. He is absorbed into a world of rush and hurry, but little speed. Most desperately he dreams of becoming one of the elite, of acquiring their manners, their privileges, their tastes—for Lagos has acquired a culture of the superstructure—skyscrapers, and all that goes with the materialistic urban culture of today. Hospitality without friendship, pleasures without enjoyment. It is a very comforting existence, for it breeds remoteness from the responsibilities of old traditions. Both for the foreigner and the Lagosian, isolation is total. The mutual contact—that remains a purely commercial proposition—smooth, mechanical, even automatic, by mutual agreement insincere—a spawning ground for international adventures before their former indigenous partners have been put temporarily out of business by military regimes. Sooner or later, the question poses itself, 'Who really owns Lagos?'

"The wealth of the nation passes through here, but where finally does it go?"

## Planned Lot Development

Lots created by planned development are, in agreement with future development proposals of the government, corporations, and private developers, to be leased for varying periods to people with the full understanding that their tenure on them is basically temporary, to relieve settlers of the major shelter problems confronting them on their first arrival in the cities.

These lots will be the landing grounds for new immigrants, and will also be the take-off grounds in the search for permanent houses when the settlers finally acquire employment and better economic standing.

During the temporary period, settlers will have the opportunity, not under the previous extremely hard conditions of shelter shortage but in an atmosphere conducive to calm, logical reasoning, to reassess their gains and losses, their thoughts and fanciful ideas of what the good life in the city means, and decide whether (a) they will be better off back in their former rural communities or (b) they can actually make a go of it in the cities.

Thus relatively little effort will be called for to convince unsuccessful settlers of the gloomy picture of frustration their future life in the city presents. At this stage highly organized, well-thought-out, really meaningful publicity should be applied tactfully. The wheels of the propaganda machine should not roll ruthlessly over the afflicted; rather, the simple fact must be recognized that the common African is a sentimental human being who values his honor, human dignity, social and economic status, self-respect, and family honor more than anything else. It must be brought to light at this juncture that many relocation housing plans in major African cities—the Central Lagos scheme, for example— failed woefully to materialize effectively because the emotional factors were not properly built into the programs. The efforts of the authorities were usually too highhanded and failed to effectively call for citizen help, participation, and co-operation.

One problem is that "temporary" structures usually become permanent. Careful planning and effective implementation devices can eliminate this tendency.

## The Problem of Relocation

How can any authority persuade the typical Lagos Island city family to evacuate their hereditary land and particularly their ancestral shrines, which are precious to them in these many ways?—

symbolic content

religious and spiritual animation and guidance

psychological conviction that the ancestors' spirits protect their kith and kin?

belief in continued wealth and prosperity if the ancestral family steadfastly refuses to part with the shrines physically belief in evil spirits that may bedevil those responsible for desecration or displacement or routing of the shrines

It is not difficult to see that the urbanized African has three distinct choices of culture. He must embrace one of these: traditional life in full measure; Western, supposedly modern, life with its total departure from the old; a blend of the traditional and the Western.

Naturally, the urbanized African mixes traditional and modern life in proportions convenient to his taste and desire. This means that he owes allegiance to two masters. In Africa, I suppose, the saying that one cannot serve two masters is not applicable because the transitional period of progressive changes can be characterized as a struggle for survival. But the Africans have an adage: "If you cannot go forward, surely you can trace your steps backwards to the point of origin, but hold fast to that good thing which is achieved already."

These are some of the psycho-social factors which impede relocation of people in housing programs. Other factors, purely economic, involve employment/income opportunities. Interruption of steady income is too great a burden to bear for local businessmen and petty traders, especially housewives who maintain in front of their mud houses their tiny stores which offer a ready market from dawn till late at night, while they can still pop in and out intermittently to attend to their domestic chores. It is economic suicide to sign up to move away to a new place; everybody knows, through experience of delay, that a housing program will normally take two to four years to function smoothly.

Also, family size may be a deterrent to relocation. Although small family units of three to six can readily move, the typical extended African family unit of fifteen or more cannot afford to move an inch.

Socio-economic status matters as well. Professional

families and other educated families with higher income move readily because they understand the situation and it is within their financial means to make a decision in favor of relocation.

But of all the factors outlined, the psycho-social are the most important, for it is these which weigh heavily on the urbanized African's mind. They constitute the core of his dilemma.

Again, the experts will do Africans a great service if they advise on how best to tackle the psycho-social problems. The methodological teaching of the art of convincing people under urbanization duress should be clearly outlined in simple terms, and how best it can be applied to housing and planning programs.

Authorities in developing countries should also understand that there is need to allot expenditures for social workers and others to assist with these problems.

## Physical Planning and Design

### CIRCULATION AND MOVEMENT

Movement of Nigerians, for example, are casual. Careful observation of Nigerians reveals that they are not used to walking long straight corridors in houses, paths, or roads. Rather, they are used to taking winding paths, roads, and detours passing by huts, houses, trees, and market places to their destinations.

Take a man going to his farm, for instance. He does not proceed by a straight road. Why? Because a straight course seems to be unending and monotonous and his farm much farther away than usual. (This is a psychological feeling which is naturally inherent in him; no one can therefore easily persuade this farmer to reach his farm by a straight road.) Then again, a winding path, as it meanders around, brings him in contact with many interesting landmarks, like the bamboo, the baobab tree, or the big mango tree from which he can always pluck some juicy fruits to eat; or even streams he can swim in or drink from; and such other natural landscape elements as have formed a substantial part of his way of life.

The fact is that for ages past the typical African village was not planned all that carefully. The earlier part of this essay outlined the development of the African village. It grew out of the instincts for defense, security, and agricultural, pastoral, or hunting needs, like an American Indian camp, with most of the exciting civic activities taking place by the banks of rivers and streams. Usually the river was a means of defense during civil wars, as it was difficult for enemies to bridge over. From the river banks the village spread farther and farther away in clusters of huts, with the chief's house nearest the river or in the center of the community, commanding a good view everywhere—a location befitting the dignity of a responsible overseer. Vast open spaces in the form of courtyards surrounded the chief's house, while other huts and houses sprang up at random around it.

There were no definite roads marked out, but there were footpaths that developed naturally, depicting the movements of villagers converging on the chief's palace for ceremonies, recreation, marketing (business), civic activities, and the like. These paths wound around the huts and the thatched houses informally; and when such villages developed and became the cities of today, these spread informally also. Such a city once established would resist physical change vigorously, for to construct a vehicular road would mean destroying valuable real properties and undertaking expensive compensation to the displaced owners. Thus, such cities would easily become overcrowded with rapid deterioration of health and sanitary standards. The eventual result would be slums, with squatter settlements developing around the periphery. An example of this is Lagos Island. But notably, the informal trend of movement of pedestrians and cyclists in the cities of Nigeria, as in Lagos, Ibadan, and Kano (Tud-un Wada), naturally enhanced the spontaneous flow of courtyard spaces into one another.

Designers should observe this element in planning traffic and circulation in African communities.

## THE ORGANIC COURTYARD

The organic courtyard has emerged as the dominant spatial element in the African village and in domestic house planning. Aside from its common recreational role, its functions are numerous and vital to African living.

The courtyard is the nucleus of the domestic house. It serves mainly for housework; and the adjoining verandah is its adjunct. Formerly it was relatively uninteresting architecturally, as its structure, usually of rammed earth filling, was not durable and became messy during rains. Nowadays conditions are improved, with the courtyard being paved of concrete.

At its four corners are receptacles permanently fixed to catch the rain water running off the roofs. Some firewood and old utensils are scattered here and there. Ropes stretch from one roof eave to the other for drying clothes in the sun. Women sit on the verandah busily spinning, sewing, making baskets, or engaging in other household industries. Here a woman is on her knees grinding pepper, and there some girls sing as they pound corn to the rhythmic thud, thud, of pestle against mortar. Sometimes there is open-air cooking, with smoke spiraling skywards. Fowls, cats, dogs, prowl about for corn and meat. As children play within the courtyard, housewives of the typical polygamous home make it their battleground when quarrels and misunderstandings arise among them. And so life goes on within the courtyard.

Aside from these common utilitarian functions, the courtyard has significant social and communal aspects.

It serves as the purdah, or harem, for Moslem housewives, who are forbidden to go out.

It serves as the playground for children. House units with interlocking courtyards of various sizes are physical controls to confine children according to their age groups within the range of parent supervision. For instance, a child under three years plays in the innermost courtyard; between three and five or six he is allowed to wander into larger courtyards according to his parents' estimate of his mental alertness to danger and the bad company of street hoodlums; when he is above six, he goes to school and is qualified to play in the more open public spaces. This means that the courtyard indirectly keeps children off the streets, especially away from automobiles.

The courtyard is slept in during the hot hours of the tropical day and night.

The courtyard and the adjoining verandah, if the weather is favorable, become hospitality and even sleeping places for new immigrants to the city, thus providing shelter for the needy who otherwise must suffer from lack of housing. The effect of this is a tendency to more intensive use, and overcrowding with its ailments. But in a way, it takes the potential squatter off the streets and away from his shack-building.

It can thus be accepted that the courtyard and the verandah are sometimes the starting points for urbanization of the new immigrant, as he socializes by meeting other members of the household around his courtyard and becomes familiar with the tenor of city life.

It "contains" the dwellers, giving them a feeling of contentment, protection, and security.

XTERIOR VIEW

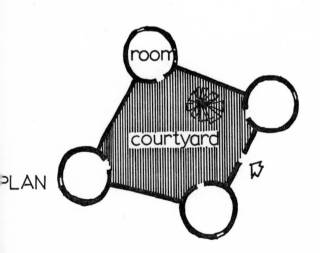

room

courtyard

PLAN

TRADITIONAL HOUSE

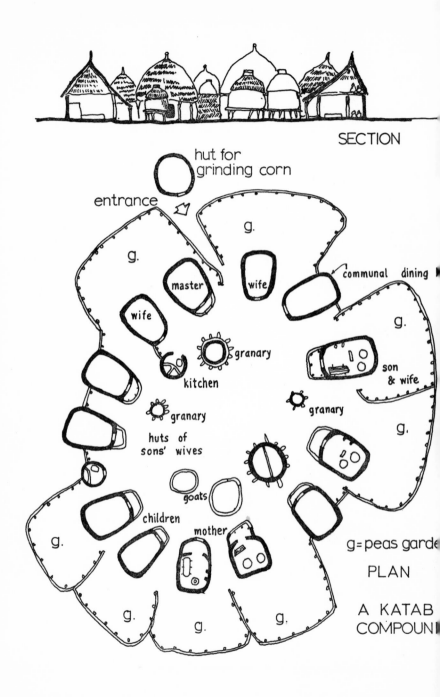

SECTION

hut for grinding corn

entrance

g.

g.

master

wife

communal dining

wife

g.

granary

son & wife

kitchen

granary

granary

huts of sons' wives

g.

goats

children

g.

mother

g = peas garden

PLAN

g.

g.

A KATAB COMPOUND

SECTION

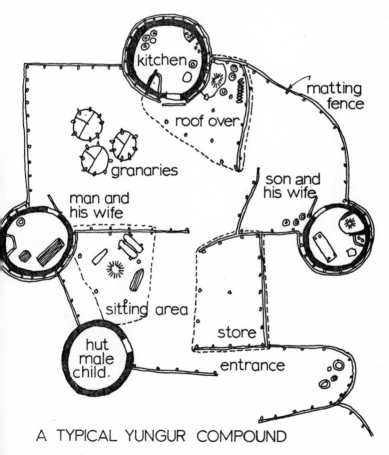

kitchen

matting fence

roof over

granaries

son and his wife

man and his wife

sitting area

hut male child.

store

entrance

A TYPICAL YUNGUR COMPOUND

OUTDOOR KITCHEN SHED

wife and children

cooking and eating

lobby 'zaure'

man

granary

_ A SMALL HAUSA RURAL COMPOUND _

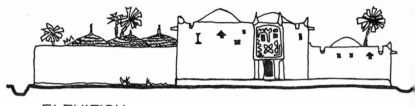

ELEVATION

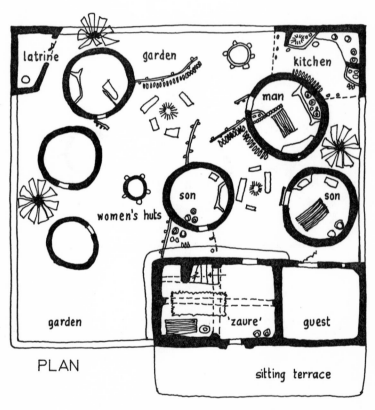

latrine garden

kitchen

man

women's huts

son

son

garden

'zaure'

guest

PLAN

sitting terrace

A HAUSA TOWN HOUSE

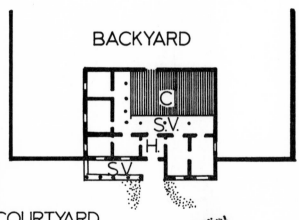

BACKYARD

C

S.V.

H.

S.V.

C = COURTYARD
H = HALL
V = SOCIAL VERANDAH

SOCIAL VERANDAH

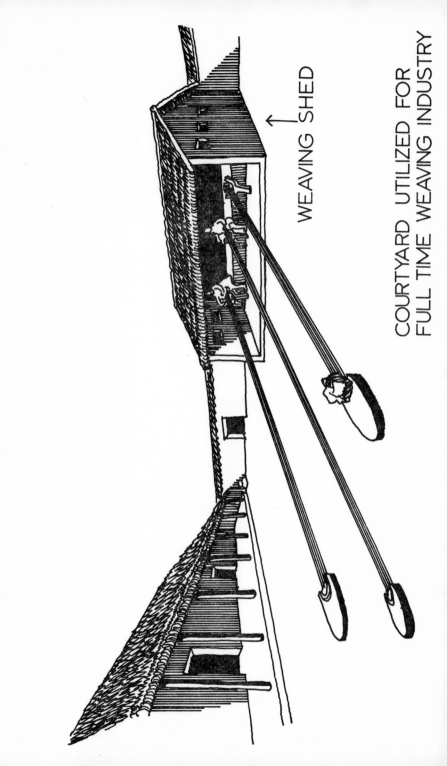

WEAVING SHED

COURTYARD UTILIZED FOR
FULL TIME WEAVING INDUSTRY

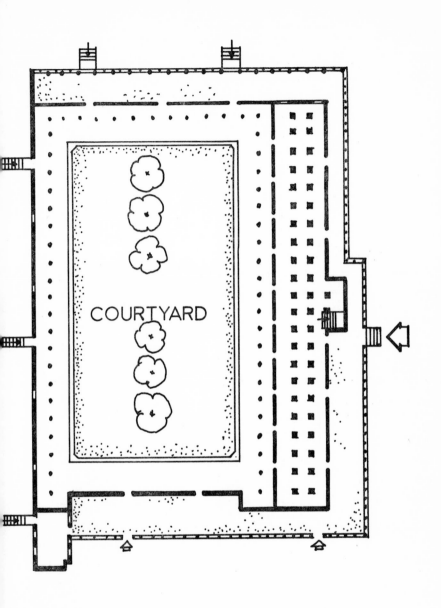

COURTYARD

ILORIN CITY CENTRAL MOSQUE
"MOSALASI JUMAH", OJA-OBA

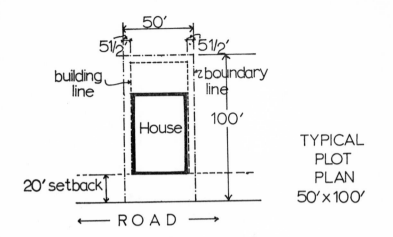

50'

5½' 5½'

building line

boundary line

House

100'

20' setback

← R O A D →

TYPICAL
PLOT
PLAN
50' x 100'

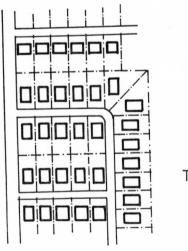

TYPICAL MODERN
LAND
SUBDIVISION

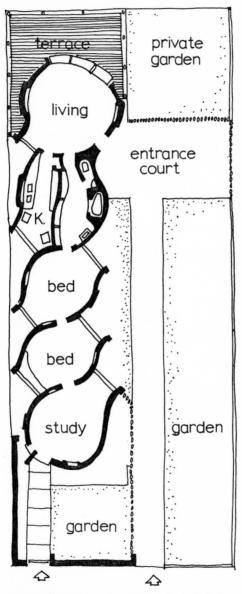

terrace

private garden

living

entrance court

K.

bed

bed

study

garden

garden

A MODERN HOUSE, LAGOS
ARCHITECT: ALLAN V. RICHARDS

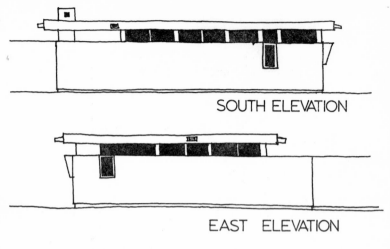

SOUTH ELEVATION

EAST ELEVATION

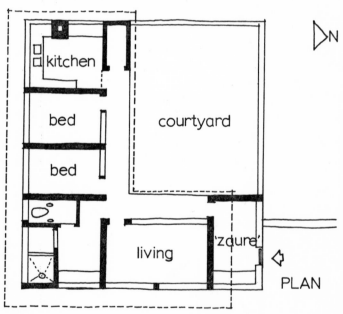

kitchen

bed

bed

courtyard

living

'zaure'

N

PLAN

A MODERN HOUSE, KADUNA
ARCHITECT: KENNETH H. MURTA

The multifunctional courtyard coupled with the informal village layout, and the informal movement of the people, to me constitute an organic whole which depicts in physical terms the people's way of life in villages and cities. It would be a sad thing if this unique structure disappeared with the transition of the old Africa to the new.

Apparently, Western ways of physical urban planning which have now been introduced have yielded not quite agreeable results. For example, Western land subdivisions have produced the following:

a) Monotony of street façades and views.

b) House types which encourage burglary because of narrow open alleys, created to allow hot, humid tropical air to flow through and around buildings for "health" reasons. In a continent of poverty, this is outrageous!

c) Zoning and building codes and regulations that do not sufficiently take into account the dire shortage of land for building houses.

d) Waste of expensive land through lavish, sprawling subdivisions which common Africans cannot afford to buy.

e) Where high-density housing should exist, town planners have shown the least consideration for it. High density does not necessarily mean high-rise apartment buildings, since it is now known through Cumbernauld New Town, in the United Kingdom, that a high density of 150 to 200 people per acre can be achieved with no difficulty. The Surulere (New Lagos) housing layout is typical of expensive land wastage. It is like reclaiming land to serve the needs of the high-income and upper middle-income elite group alone—an idea contrary to the initial objective of the housing program. However commendable the healthy physical appearance of the layout may be, at the expense of the poor majority.

I am convinced that the courtyard has a most significant role to play in shaping the new African urban physical environment. The standard subdivision lot of 50 by 100 (5000 square feet) is beyond the purchasing power of the common African. He could still have his household live around a courtyard on a lot of total dimension 25 by 40 feet (1000 square feet) or 30 by 30 feet (900 square feet)—an area one-fifth, or less, of what he is now required to buy if he is to have his own plot of land on a freehold basis. Architects and planners should work out acceptable modules for land subdivision in conformity with the purchasing power of the commoners' incomes. If this is done, squatting will diminish at least five times, and overcrowding and epidemics will decrease enormously. Architects and planners should propose high-density housing of at least four or five stories in such a land-scarce city as Lagos. Careful thought should be given to cluster development so that several families may share a courtyard; and to cheaper construction methods, such as cross-wall, load-bearing wall construction. These should aim at providing the roof and the skeleton structural framework for housing structures so that dwellers can complete their houses, flats, and units at their own pace, within their own financial capability.

This will relieve the urbanized African of much of the dilemma confronting him in securing shelter, and shelter of the modern and durable type. Blending the old with modern architecture and planning will satisfy his middle-of-the-road attitude in his search for a satisfactory new African environment—one that relates to historical development of his past and at the same time points to the new, modern future.

As for the architectural decoration and ornamentation of his house, that is left to his own personal choice—whether it be conservative or abstract "Picasso" style.

In addition, building codes which prescribe excessive minimum sizes of rooms for tropical houses should be revised. Sizes should be reasonably reduced to conform with the people's way of life and well-thought-out traffic layout and sanitary facilities. It should be noted that Africans *do not want and do not like to live in large numbers in one room*. The housing shortage and poor economic conditions necessitate the practice. I am sure this condition will change for the better through expert planning that reaches the local level.

## CLIMATIC COMFORT

In the confusion of the housing shortage, climatic comfort is usually ignored by the urbanized African. He can forego this during the search for shelter. In short, the urbanized African, used to the scorching tropical sun all his life anyway, does not think twice about climatic comfort. Thus, it is a luxury and of minor importance to commoners. The rich count it a strong design factor in housing; but what is the proportion of the rich? Negligible.

Unfortunately, most foreign experts and practitioners give more emphasis and publicity to climatic comfort than to the basic quantitative need for shelter. I shall not discuss climatic comfort because I do not think it is a major problem of housing and urbanization in the tropics at the moment or even of the near future. (Maxwell Fry and Jane Drew, with vast experience in tropical architectural practice, have contributed immensely to climatic solutions in the tropics around the world. They have admirably documented their knowledge in *Tropical Architecture, Architecture in the Humid Zones,* and *Village Housing in the Tropics.* I recommend these books highly.)

## Minimizing the Spread of Squatters

The following proposals are made for land reform and control of subdivision design:

1. Replan layout of new lands.
2. Revise land sizes for sale, rent, lease, etc.
3. Revise building codes and regulations.
4. Encourage the public to adapt architect-designed house plans.
5. The architect-designed plans should reflect—
    a) Flexibility, for changes.
    b) Quick erection.
    c) Cheap materials and low building costs.
    d) Quick readiness and availability for purchase.
    e) Minimum skilled labor required for construction.
    f) House sizes in relation to family sizes and family expansion.
    g) House types in relation to owners' types of jobs.
    h) Income levels of owners.
    i) Climatic orientation—sun and breeze.
    j) Easy accessibility by pedestrians.
    k) Courtyard planning on a smaller scale, in accord with "containment" and the social aspects of the people's living habits.
6. Consider major and secondary transportation types, routes, and media.
7. Create a very flexible zoning ordinance that will reflect the people's daily customary activities of living and working, e.g., local stalls built into house verandahs.
8. Observe traditional village characteristics, e.g., compactness, recreation, and socials, while making new community plans.
9. Plans must be so designed as to be capable of effectua-

tion in stages, and of urban renewal in stages as the governnment's economic decisions permit.

10. Houses may be designed to last for a certain anticipated life span, but with a little higher quality and durability, should there be an adverse change in government policy.

## Methods of Implementation

### Community Action

Encouragement of community action for community development, and the initiation of self-help housing programs at minimum cost.

### Re-evaluation of Land

Re-evaluation of land with a view to encouraging transfer of industries to the urban fringe. Since employment location is a strong factor in Africa today and will continue to be, people will naturally tend to gravitate to new industrial centers in establishing residence. The expert should devise a crude transportation model. This human pattern of behavior could be reinforced in organized, planned land use for the communities in question.

### Taxation

Review of the tax structure of land and buildings—i.e., taxes in cities to be much higher than in rural and urban-fringe areas.

In Latin America, planning offices tend to operate as authorities for restrictive protection of certain community values instead of performing in the larger scope of a master plan.

Government could buy land and formulate a framework within which people could buy and operate. The area would be declared as a "public concern" with a specified tax value, e.g., 25 per cent of land cost, to be paid. This is a method of "conversion" of rural to urban land. Uruguay and Chile have this system. It checks unruly land speculation. Germany after the war taxed land heavily with practically no tax on developments, thus promoting rapid reconstruction of the country. This tax system could be reversed after a city had achieved good recovery.

Experts should help African planning authorities and government real-property assessors to devise an acceptable tax framework. The government could accept surplus products in lieu of tax revenue in poor areas. The surplus could be exported.

High taxing of commodities or land in slums is objectionable because it will mean taking money from impoverished slum dwellers to develop their own slum areas. The slum slogan "Pay taxes and die" could well develop, with staggering political repercussions.

## SHORT-RANGE PLANS

Long-range development plans of five to six years are fine for projects of broad scope. But unfortunately beneficial results do not emerge until some years after execution of the plans. This is harmful to poor countries, as in Africa, where the need for cash is stressed everywhere, and especially when the countries lack required initial capital.

I therefore feel that serious consideration should be given to the introduction of short-range plans. These would consist of community-improvement package programs, e.g., for schools, housing, clinics, and factories that could make use of available raw materials and thus provide employment for people, with immediate financial returns realized—plywood, cement, canning fruits and vegetables, and refrigeration to avoid waste of food. Even these improvement programs should in turn have built-in "impact projects" which will make use of the abundant local skills and crafts in a modern factory way, e.g., leather and dyeing, as at Kano, weaving of "Kente" cloths, smithing, and tailoring, backed by crash in-service training to develop skills.

The government or the private organizations responsible for sponsoring such programs could aim at investing small capital only—perhaps money from shares offered for purchase to the public. If the community, through detailed planning, could be involved effectively, profits will flow out much sooner than expected. Trading and home industry have characterized the Nigerians, regardless of tribal differences.

## REGIONAL ECONOMIC PLANNING TO CHECK
## MIGRATION AT THE RURAL SOURCE

CASH-ECONOMY AGRICULTURE. People prefer to earn cash, and want cash by all means. Why? Because modern African societies have emphasized development programs and higher social values not only on paper but in practice, taking into consideration, above all, (a) The need for education at all levels of learning. For example, Nigeria devotes from 25 to 35 per cent of the financial costs of her program to education. (b) The need for improved shelter and living standards. (c) The need for better health facilities. (d) The aspiration of most Africans to obtain lucrative employment.

Unfortunately the lucrative jobs are still off the farm, in offices, institutions, and industry. Responsibilities at state, community, and private domestic levels have grown incredibly when compared with what obtained twenty years ago, before political independence.

A study in depth of existing social organizations should reveal detailed sampling of people's attitudes, convictions, behavior, aspirations, abilities, and willingness to work and to spend their money. The will to work and to progress is necessary for the development of agriculture. The development of improved, mechanized agriculture as a sizable economic base on which stronger local centers can be created from existing strong centers or villages of importance can be a profitable venture. Governments and private corporations could capitalize on this.

Countries today need developed agriculture. Countries which lack it are usually at the mercy of those which lend them aid.

In most African countries agriculture is the mainstay of the economy. In Nigeria, 90 per cent of the farming is done by hand because of the lack of mechanized agricultural tools and equipment. Needless to say, it is low-yield.

Public enlightenment in the use of fertilizers should be expanded. The use of mixed fertilizers in Nigeria in a 1963 study by Arthur D. Little yielded much better products. An investment in mixed fertilizers would yield 15 per cent profit annually.

There is an abundance of unskilled labor, while the technical manpower that will be needed in the future calls for a massive effort in Africa and a free movement of scientists and technicians across national boundaries, though there are not yet enough to staff key control institutes. There is need of improved transportation media—railroads and highways—and communications—telephone, radio, television.

The current experiment of agricultural modernization through co-operative "farm settlements," as in Western Nigeria, should be expanded and developed into large-scale programs. The idea is to induce young Nigerians and experienced farmers who might ordinarily migrate to the cities to remain on the farm and become the vanguard of modern, cash-economy agriculture.[3] This will check the influx of immigrants into existing large cities right from the source, and thus indirectly mitigate the dilemma of urbanization.

Regional economic planning should be carefully studied in order to arrest the problem of urbanization at the rural sources, and in order to generate new urban regional centers in the hinterland rather than only on the coast.

### SELF-HELP

The communal type of living at both village and city levels makes self-help programs easy to carry out, e.g., E.C.A. training programs in Ethiopia, Kenya, and Latin America. The values of self-help can be realized through reason, education, training, and effective administration. The programs should aim at convincing the village people who are dissatisfied with their cash-starved communities and whose alternative thus far has been to migrate to the cities to establish farm settlements. Villagers will be persuaded to stay behind and realize that they can create a good life for themselves in the villages. At the same time new employment opportunities will be created for youngsters leaving school who naturally tend to migrate to cities, causing acute unemployment.

---

[3] *U.N. Technical Assistance Newsletter,* Jan.–Feb. 1963, p. 4.

# Major Impediments to Urbanization and
# Housing in the Developing Countries

## Imbalance Between Population
## and Economic Development

The statement ". . . urbanized societies, in which a majority of the people live crowded together in towns and cities, represent a new and fundamental step in man's social evolution"[4] is realistic. From 1950 to 1960 the world's population growth rate was 2 per cent and the population growth rate of the developing countries was 3.6 per cent. If this increase were to remain the same, the fraction of the world's people living in cities with a population of 100,000 or larger would have half as much people again by 1999.

It is best to define urbanization here as the proportion of the total population concentrated in urban settlement. It is not simply the growth of cities. Since the total population is composed of both urban population and rural, the "proportion urban" is a function of both of them.[5] Kingsley Davis in the introduction to his study of the urbanization of human population says that ". . . accordingly cities can grow with-

---

[4] See *Cities* (A Scientific American Book), pp. 1-14; also Charles Abrams, *Man's Struggle for Shelter in an Urbanizing World* (Cambridge, Mass.: M.I.T. Press).

[5] *Report of the Ad Hoc Group of Experts on Housing and Urban Development* (United Nations Publication).

out any urbanization, provided that the rural population grows at an equal or greater rate." The proportion of people in cities can rise because—

a) Rural settlements grow larger and are reclassified as towns or cities.
b) The excess of births over deaths is greater in the cities than in the country.
c) On balance, people move from the country to the cities.

The last two factors have accounted for the urban population explosion, especially in Africa.

Modern urbanization is best understood in terms of its connection with economic growth. It can thus be observed as a cycle through which nations go in their transition from an agrarian to an industrial society. I am inclined to believe that the increase in population of a city is less of a problem, provided the population does not increase more than the per capita income.

Adequate economic employment for the population will dispel the fear we now have of the cities. With good and steady incomes, accompanied by appropriate urban land reforms, people will be able to buy houses; thus housing problems will be minimized.

## Lack of Constructive and Co-ordinated Planning

National development plans and national policy and legislation for housing and urban development should reflect a bold design concept and the courage to take a dare. Venezuela entered where angels fear to tread and is successful even at such a precarious level of social and economic development as exists in Latin America.[6]

---

[6] John Friedman, *Venezuela from Doctrine to Dialogue* (Syracuse, N.Y.: Syracuse Univ. Press, 1965).

If developing countries will execute such an effective combined program of national development, the yoke of underdevelopment will be lifted at a much faster rate.

## *Shortage of Staff*

There is a great need for education and training of personnel, of technicians in all fields, e.g., planners, architects, engineers, economists, sociologists, administrators, statisticians. It is usually difficult to obtain statistical data from the developing countries because of lack of trained personnel. How can experts produce accurate forecasts as in the United States, the United Kingdom, France, etcetera, with figures usually derived from extremely rough estimation and insufficient description of existing conditions in the countries they deal with?

The need for the training of architects and planners for the implementation of programs has been widely discussed elsewhere. The professionals can translate national development policies into physical realities.[7]

There should be a program for teaching the people of developing countries the technical know-how in practical ways by which they can help themselves to improve their living standards to the modern level.

---

[7] See, for example, Eric Carlson and Walter D. Harris, *Study on International Housing* (Subcommittee on Housing Committee on Banking and Currency, U.S. Senate), Chap. C, par. 10.

## Insufficient Study of the Economics and Financing of Housing[8]

The economics and financing of housing in developing countries is either not studied at all or not studied thoroughly. The developed countries, of course, equipped with modern techniques, have somehow conquered knowledge of this field for themselves. But I should say that the hazards created by the extremely rapid process of urbanization make the field more complicated to study and master in the developing countries. It will require teaming together the efforts of experts from advanced countries and of indigenous trained personnel of the developing countries who may be more familiar than foreigners with local conditions.

Careful attention should be given to how the people's savings and resources can be mobilized and channeled for housing purposes, through savings-and-loan systems, cooperatives, credit unions, and other techniques.

## Lack of Research on Indigenous Building Materials and Methods of Improvement

The governments of developing countries seem to be overwhelmed with modernization and are so preoccupied with prestigious programs that they neglect to develop well-equipped research institutes devoted to improvement and modernization of construction, materials, and methods in housing, even though some native practices and materials may be crude and obsolete.

---

[8] Charles Abrams, *op. cit.*, Chaps. 5, 11.

Foreign advisers, through the United Nations or other agencies, should help stress the importance of this sector of national development. The blessing that housing and urban development can receive through research is unlimited.[9]

## Incommensurate Allocation of Government Funds

Governments of developing countries are reluctant to put money into housing and urban development. They regard housing as a major problem but allocate minor estimates to it in their development programs. Whatever are the reasons behind such a diffident attitude, whether economic or social, they should remember that a stitch in time saves nine and that the complex problem of housing and urbanization is best arrested or curbed in its embryo stage. Negligence in facing up to this responsibility is simply a postponement of the worries to future generations.

Money alone, however, is not the answer. It requires a greater effort of commitment and resolution.

---

[9] *Ibid.*, p. 208; also *Report on the Ad Hoc Group of Experts on Housing and Urban Development*, Chap. 2 (b) (v).

# References

Of the literature examined, the following items have made appreciable contributions to the formation of my opinions and suggestions outlined in this book.

Aboyade, O. In *Nigerian Journal of Economic and Social Studies* (Ibadan Univ. Press, Ibadan, Nigeria), March 1967.

Abrams, Charles. *The City Is the Frontier*. New York: Harper & Row, 1965.

———. *Man's Struggle for Shelter in an Urbanizing World*. Cambridge: Mass. Inst. Tech. Press.

——— and others. *Metropolitan Lagos*. United Nations Publication, April 27, 1964.

Beuscher, J. H. *Land Use Controls*. Madison, Wisc.: College Printing & Typing, 1964.

Beyer, Glenn H. *Housing: A Factual Analysis*. New York: Macmillan, 1958.

*Building Research Station Notes on Tropics*. Garston, England: B.R.S.

*Cities* (A Scientific American Book). New York: Alfred Knopf, 1965.

Croxton, F. E., and D. Cowden. *Applied General Statistics*. New York: Prentice-Hall, 1963.

Drew, Jane. *Village Housing in the Tropics*. London: L. Humphries, 1947.

Friedman, John. *Venezuela from Doctrine to Dialogue*. Syracuse, N.Y. Syracuse Univ. Press, 1965.

Fry, Maxwell, and Jane Drew. *Tropical Architecture*. New York: Reinhold, 1964.

———. *Tropical Architecture in the Humid Zones.* New York: Reinhold, 1956.

Gallion and Eisner. *The Urban Pattern.* New York: Van Nostrand, 1963.

Goodman, Percival and Paul. *Communitas.* New York: Vintage Books, 1960.

Green, Philip Jr. *Cases for Law and Administration.* Chapel Hill: Univ. of North Carolina, 1962.

Haar, Charles. *Land Use Planning.* Boston: Little, Brown, 1959.

*Handbook for Social Research in Urban Areas.* UNESCO Publication.

*Housing in Africa.* United Nations Publication, Sept. 1965.

*Housing through Non-Profit Organizations.* United Nations Publication.

*Journal of the Estate Agents Institute* (London).

*Journal of the Royal Institute of British Architects* (London).

*Journal of the Royal Institution of Chartered Surveyors* (London).

*Journal of the Town Planning Institute of Britain* (London).

Koenigsberger, O. H. *Building Costs in Nigeria.* United Nations Publication, June 15, 1962.

*Lagos Building Codes and Regulations.* Lagos, Nigeria: L.C.C., 1962.

London *Times,* Jan. 18. 1967.

Lynch, Kevin. *The Image of the City.* Cambridge: Mass. Inst. Tech. Press, 1960.

*Manual on Self-help Housing.* United Nations Publication.

Meyerson, Terret, and Wheaton. *Housing, People and Cities.* New York: McGraw-Hill, 1962.

*Modern African Studies,* Vol. 4. No. 4. Cambridge Univ. Press.

Mumford, Lewis. *The City in History.* New York: Harcourt, Brace & World, 1961.

Murta, K. H. *Traditional Domestic Architecture of Northern Nigeria.* England: Sheffield Univ. Library.

*Nigerian Ministry of Information Bulletin.* Lagos: Fed. Min. of Information.

Ojo, G. J. A. In *Nigerian Journal of Geographers* (Ibadan Univ. Press, Ibadan, Nigeria), June 1966.

Okin, T. A. *Historical and Architectural Development of Ilorin City*. Zaria, Nigeria: Ahmadu Bello Univ., 1960.

*Report of the Ad Hoc Group of Experts on Housing and Urban Development*. United Nations Publication.

Rowan, Jan C. In *Progressive Architecture*, April 1965.

*Study of International Housing*. Washington, D.C.: U.S. Govt. Printing Office.

*Traffic in Towns*. London: H.M. Stationery Office, 1963.

*West Africa Magazine* (London).

*World Housing Conditions and Estimated Housing Requirements*. United Nations Publication.